Young Children's Activity Guide 1

Copyright 2008
Time to Sign, Inc.
211 4th Avenue
Indialantic, FL 32903
(321) 726-9466
contact@timetosign.com
www.timetosign.com

Name: _____

ANT HILL MAZE

Directions: Help the ant find it's way from the ant hill and through the maze so that it can get to the apple.

2.

"Apples and Bananas"
(Original Author Unknown, Illistraions Copyright 2002 Time to Sign, Inc.)

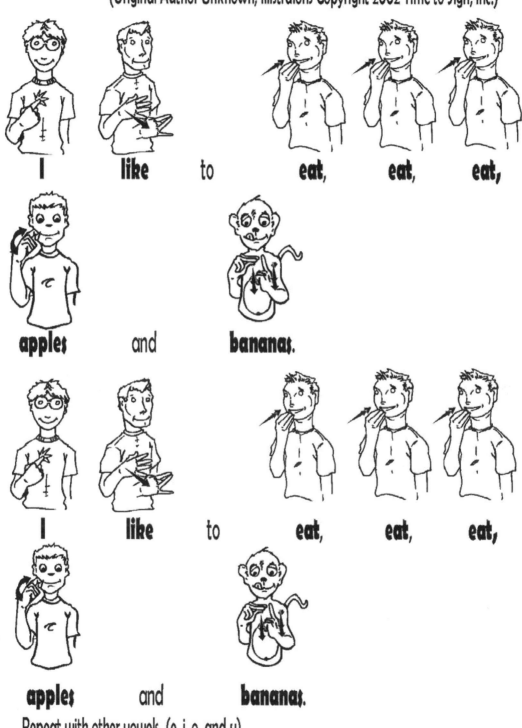

I like to eat, eat, eat, apples and bananas.

I like to eat, eat, eat, apples and bananas.

Repeat with other vowels (e, i, o, and u).

3.

Bb

bumble bee

bear

Name: _____

Letter Search

Directions: Circle the letter Bb in the sign language letters below.

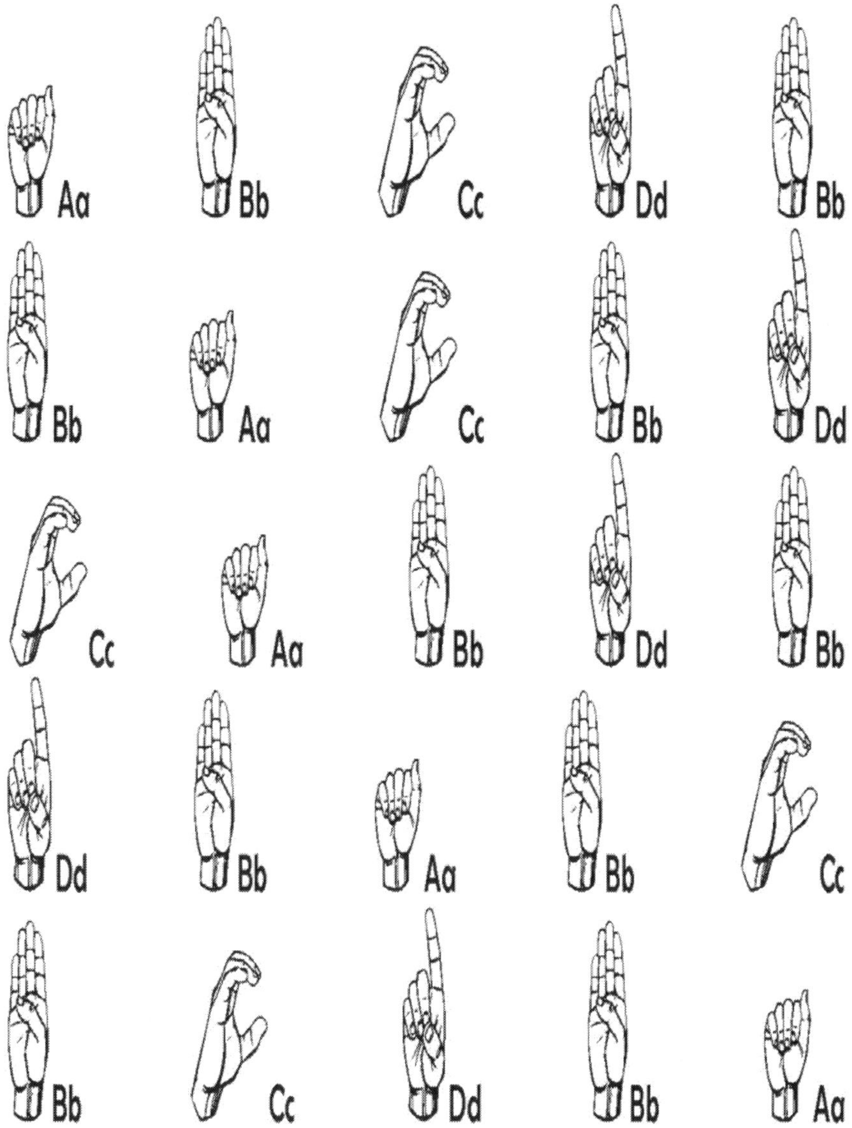

Aa	Bb	Cc	Dd	Bb
Bb	Aa	Cc	Bb	Dd
Cc	Aa	Bb	Dd	Bb
Dd	Bb	Aa	Bb	Cc
Bb	Cc	Dd	Bb	Aa

Name: _____

MATCH GAME

Directions: Draw a line connecting the sign language to the correct picture.

8.

Name: _____

Calendar Color's

Directions: Color the winter months blue, spring months green, summer months yellow, and fall months red

January

Februray

March

April

May

June

July

August

September

October

November

December

"Seven Days"
(Traditional, Illustrations Copyright©2002 Time to Sign, Inc.)

Dd

dog

duck

Name: _____

MATCH GAME

Directions: Draw a line connecting the sign language to the correct picture.

Name: _____

Review Page

Directions: Write the first letter of each word next to the picture.

_____   _____

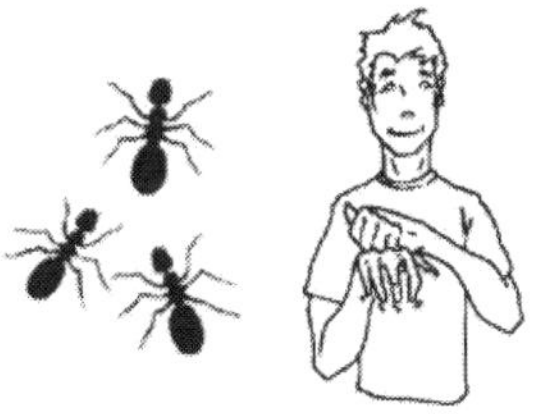

_____   _____

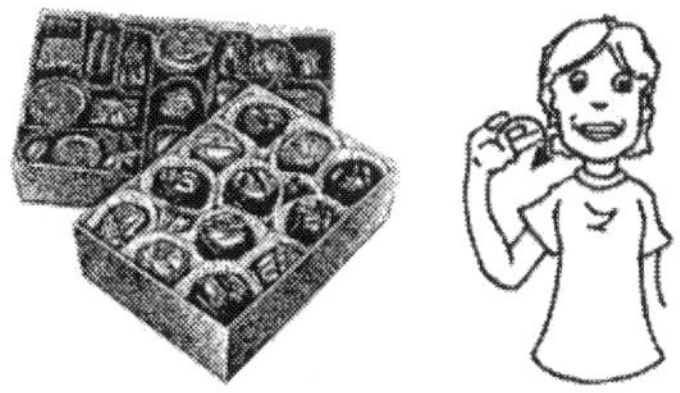

_____   _____

_____   _____

13.

Name: _____

Alphabet Soup

Directions: Find and Circle all of the E's in the bowl of soup.

15.

Ff
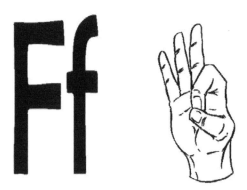

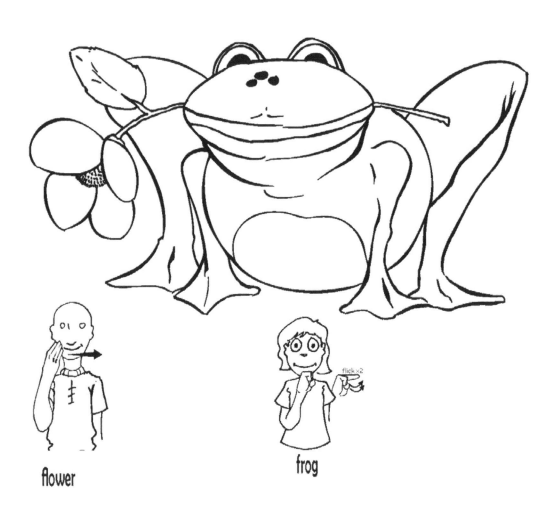

flower   frog

"Flutter, Flutter Butterfly"
(Original Author Unknown, tune of "Twinkle, Twinkle Little Star", Illustrations Copyright 2004 Time to Sign, Inc.)

Name: _____

Feed the Frog

Directions: Help the frog find his food by drawing a line to connect his toung to the F flying around him.

18.

Gg

garden

goat

Name: _____

Goat Maze

Directions: Help the goat get through the garden.

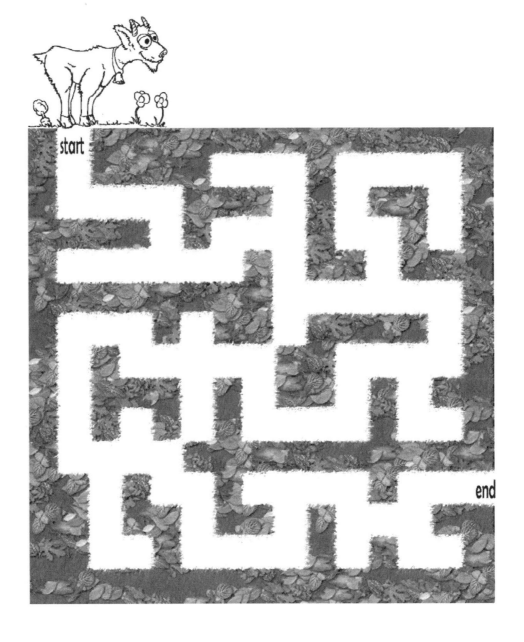

Hh

horse

house

Name: _____

Alphabet Soup

Directions: Find all of the H's and circle them.

22.

Name: _____

Review Page

Directions: Write the first letter of each word next to the picture.

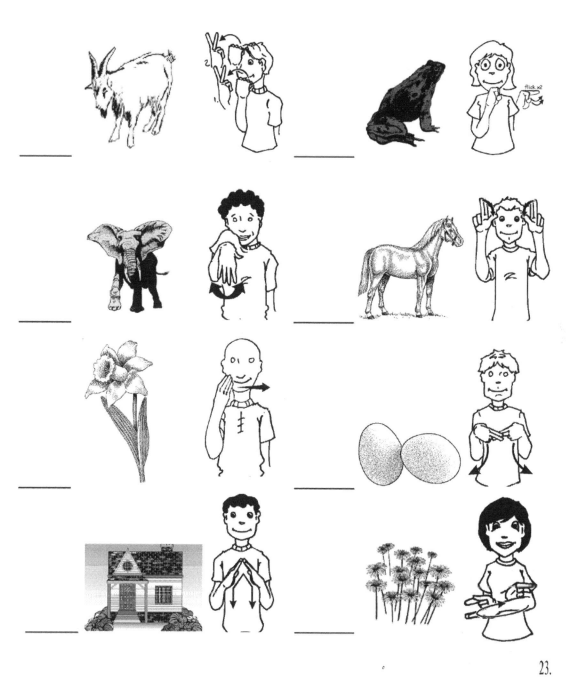

23.

Name: _____

Signing With Numbers

Directions: Draw a line connecting the number with it's sign.

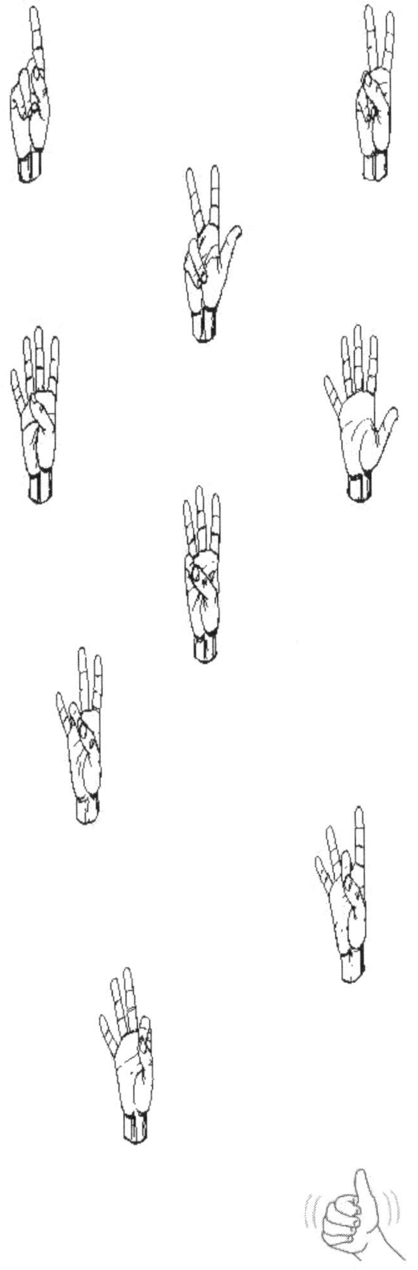

9 7

3

5

2

8

1 4

6

10

24.

Ii

ice cream

iguana

Name: _____

Iguana Maze

Directions: Help the Iguana get off of the ice into the warmth of the sun.

Jj

jaguar

jacket

Name: _____

MATCH GAME

Directions: Draw a line connecting the sign language to the correct picture.

28.

Kk

kite

kangaroo

Name: _____

Find The K's

Directions: Find and circle all of the Kk's in the picture below.

30.

Name: _____

Lovely Lady Bug

Directions: Draw 10 L's on each of the lady bug's wings to create spots.
Color the finished lady bug.

Name: _____

Review Page

Directions: Write the first letter of each word next to the picture.

Name: _____

Emotions: How do you feel today?

Directions: draw a face depicting the emotion signed below.

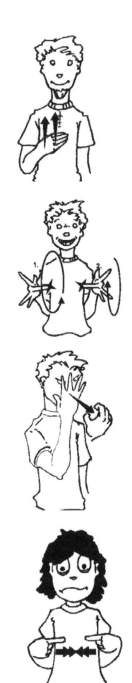

34.

"Do You Know the Muffin Man"
(Traditional, Illustrations Copyright 2003 Time to Sign, Inc.)

Do **you** **know** the **muffin** **man,**

The **muffin** **man,** The **muffin** **man,**

Do **you** **know** the **muffin** **man,**

Who **lives** on **Drury** (d-handshape) **Lane.** (repeat song)

Name: _____

Letter Search

Directions: Circle the letter Mm in the signlanguage letters below.

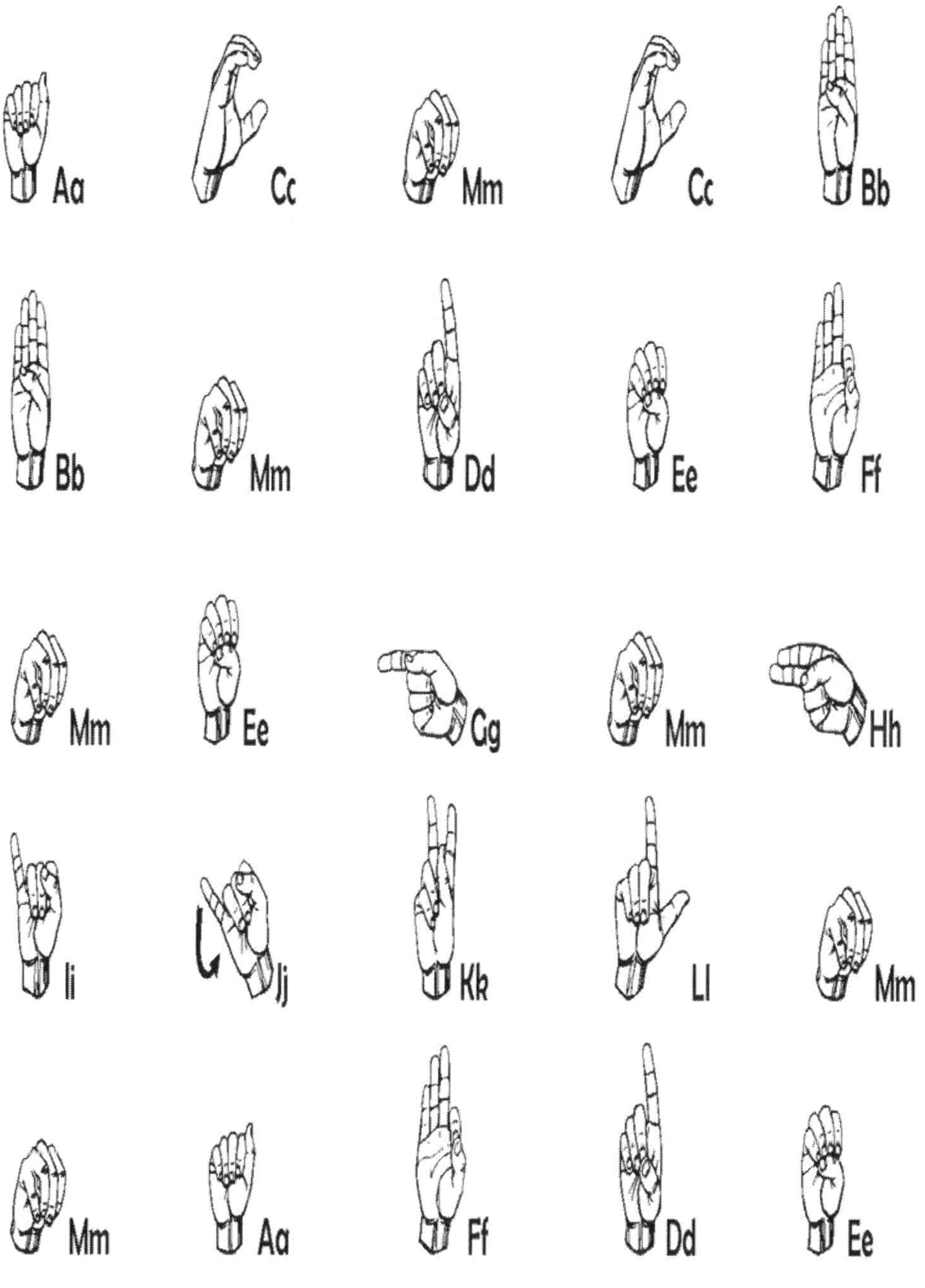

Aa	Cc	Mm	Cc	Bb
Bb	Mm	Dd	Ee	Ff
Mm	Ee	Gg	Mm	Hh
Ii	Jj	Kk	Ll	Mm
Mm	Aa	Ff	Dd	Ee

Name _____

Food Pyramid Match Up

Directions: Draw a line from the sign to the food group that matches it.

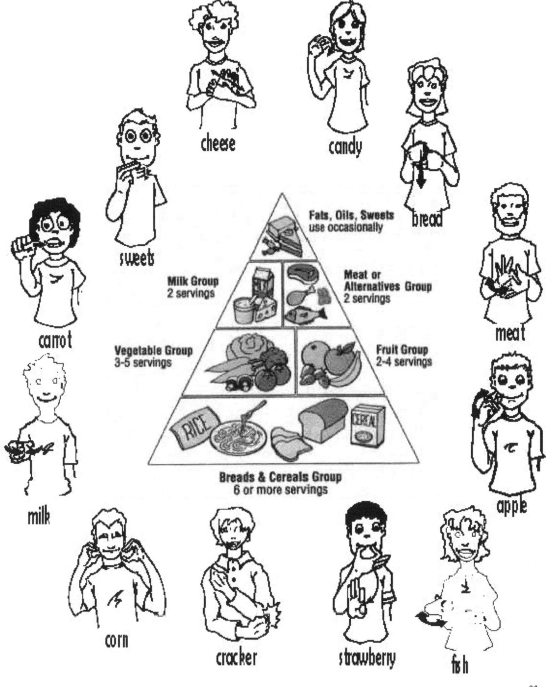

Oo

octopus

owl

40.

Blank For Cut And Paste

1

Name: _____

Olly the Octopus

Directions: Cut out objects on the previous page that begin with O and paste them to the tenticals on the octopus below.

Name: _____

MATCH GAME

Directions: Draw a line connecting the sign language to the correct picture.

44.

Pp

peach

pig

45.

Name: _____

Letter Search

Directions: Circle the letter Pp in the signlanguage letters below.

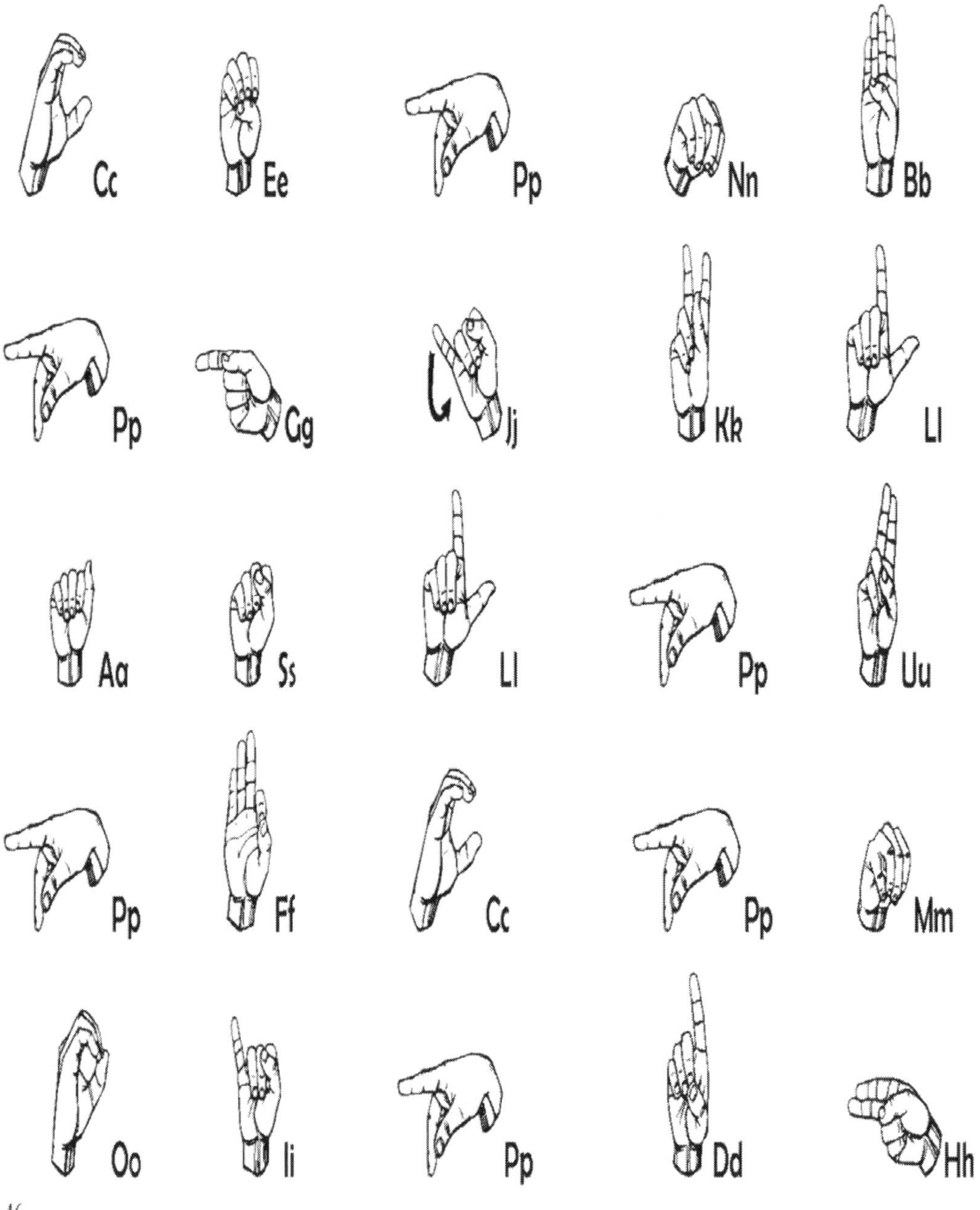

Cc	Ee	Pp	Nn	Bb
Pp	Gg	Jj	Kk	Ll
Aa	Ss	Ll	Pp	Uu
Pp	Ff	Cc	Pp	Mm
Oo	Ii	Pp	Dd	Hh

Name: _____

Review Page

Directions: Write the first letter of each word next to the picture.

Where Are My Pets?

Copyright©2003 Time to Sign, inc.

"Where is kitty?"

"Here I am!"

"How are you today?"

"Very tired, I say."

"Where is puppy?"

"Here I am!"

"How are you today?"

"Very silly, I say."

"Where is fishy?"

"Here I am!"

"How are you today?"

"Very thirsty, I say."

"Where is birdie?"

"Here I am!"

"How are you today?"

"Very happy, I say."

"Where is bunny?"   "Here I am!"

"How are you today?"   "Very excited, I say."

"Where is turtle?"   "Here I am!"

"How are you today?"   "Very grumpy, I say."

"Where is snake?"

"Here I am!"

"How are you today?"

"Very angry, I say."

"Where is mouse?"

"Here I am!"

"How are you today?"

"Very scared, I say."

"Where is horse?"

"Here I am!"

"How are you today?"

"Very hungry, I say."

"Where are my pets?"

"Here we are!"

"What would you like to do today?"   "Let's go play!"

"Please and Thank You"
(Author Unknown, Illustrations Copyright 2002 Time to Sign, Inc.)

Please and **thank you,** **please** and **thank you.**

Magic **words,** **magic** **words.**

Everyone should **use** them, **everyone** should **use** them.

Everyday, everyday.

Name: _____

Manners Match

Directions: Draw a line matching all of the manner signs with the manner words.

thank you

please

excuse me

welcome

may I

Name: _____

Q's for the Queen

Directions: Draw Q's on the Queen's crown to create her diamonds.

Name: _____

Letter Search

Directions: Circle the letter Rr in the signlanguage letters below.

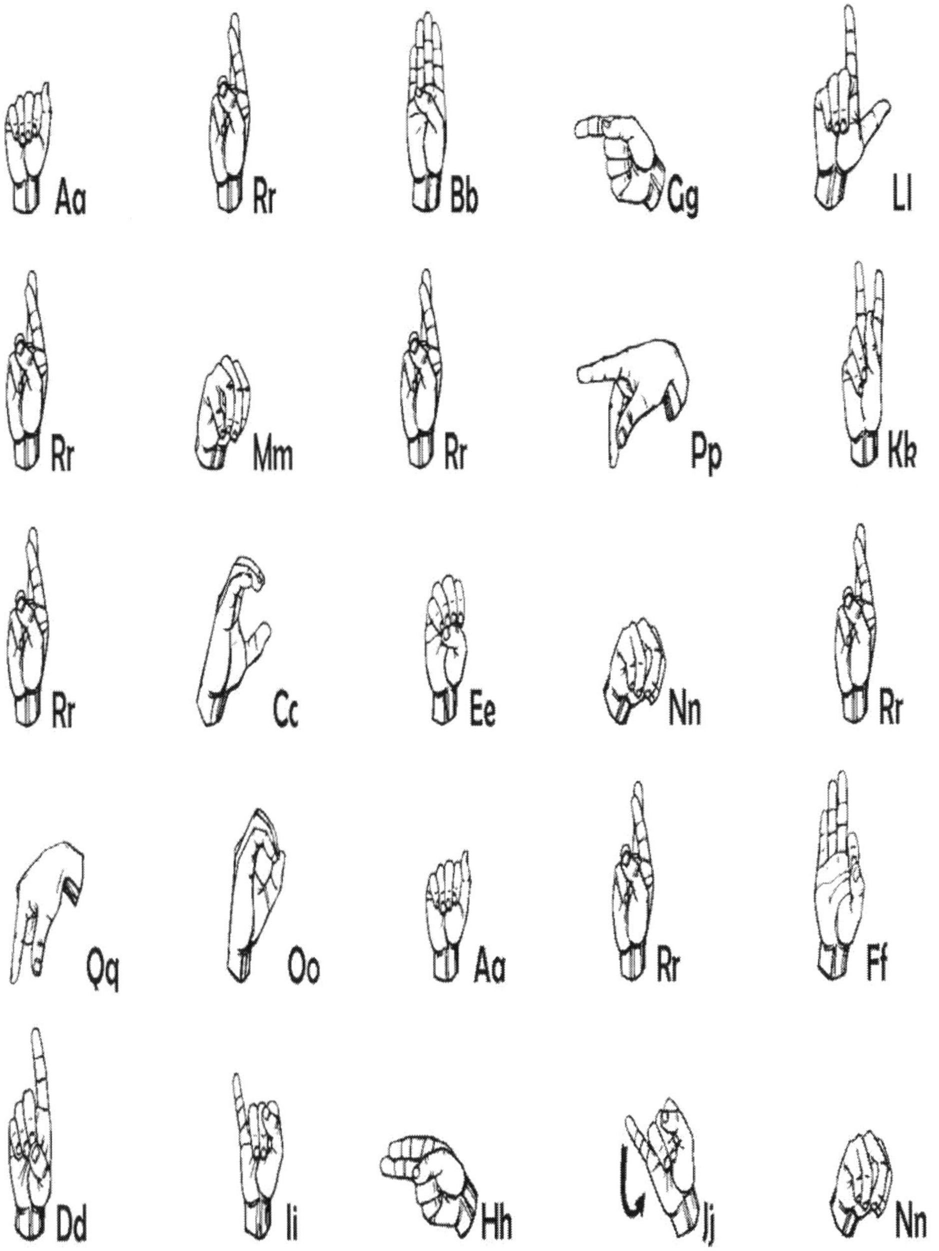

Aa	Rr	Bb	Gg	Ll
Rr	Mm	Rr	Pp	Kk
Rr	Cc	Ee	Nn	Rr
Qq	Oo	Aa	Rr	Ff
Dd	Ii	Hh	Jj	Nn

"Mr. Sun"
(Traditional, Illustrations Copyright 2002 Time to Sign, Inc.)

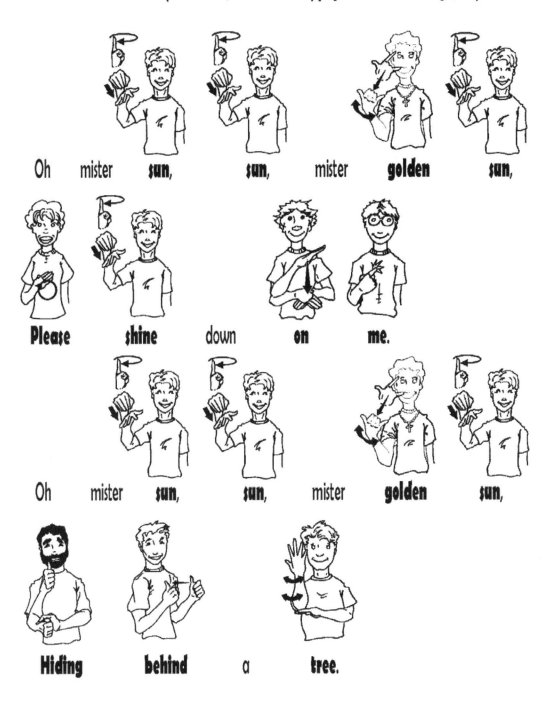

These **little** **children** are **asking** **you**,

To **please** **come** **out**

So **we** **can** **play** **with** **you**

Oh mister **sun,** **sun,** mister **golden** **sun,**

Please **shine** down on,

BLANK FOR CUT AND PASTE

Name: _____

Cut and Paste

Directions: Cut out the sign language words on the previous page and paste them on top of the corresponding pictures.

Tt

tiger

train

Name: _____

Hidden Picture

Directions: Find and circle the T's hidden in the train.

67.

Name: _____

Review Page

Directions: Write the first letter of each word next to the picture.

Name: _____

Color Match

Directions: Draw a line connecting the color sign to the object most likely representing the sign.

69.

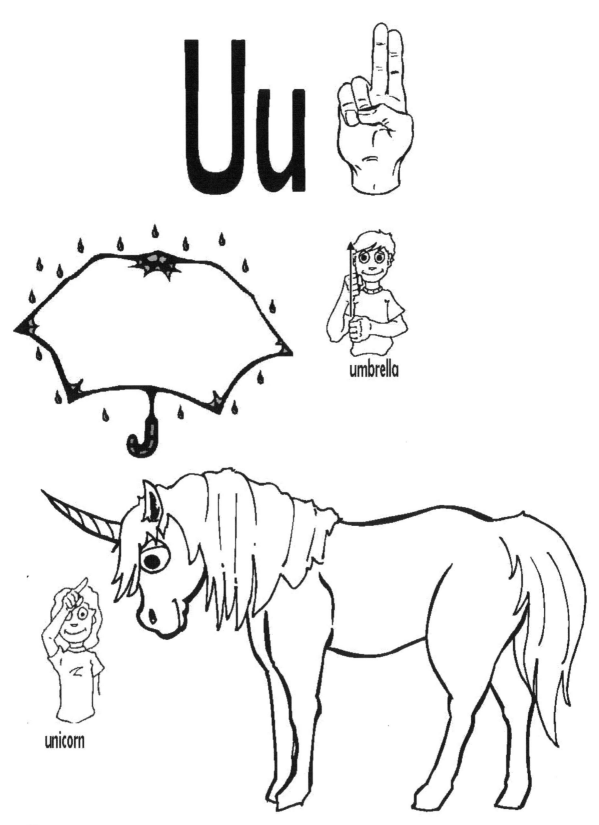

Name: _____

MATCH GAME

Directions: Draw a line connecting the sign language to the correct picture.

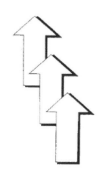

Uu

71.

Vv

vulture

violin

Name: _____

Hidden Picture

Directions: Find and circle the V signs that are hidden in the vultures wings.

73.

Ww

water

whale

Blank For Cut And Paste

76.

Name: _____

Cut and Paste

Directions: Cut out the sign language words from the previous page and paste them below the corresponding objects on this page.

Xx

xylophone

x-ray fish

78.

Name: _____

Letter Search

Directions: Circle the letter Xx in the signlanguage letters below.

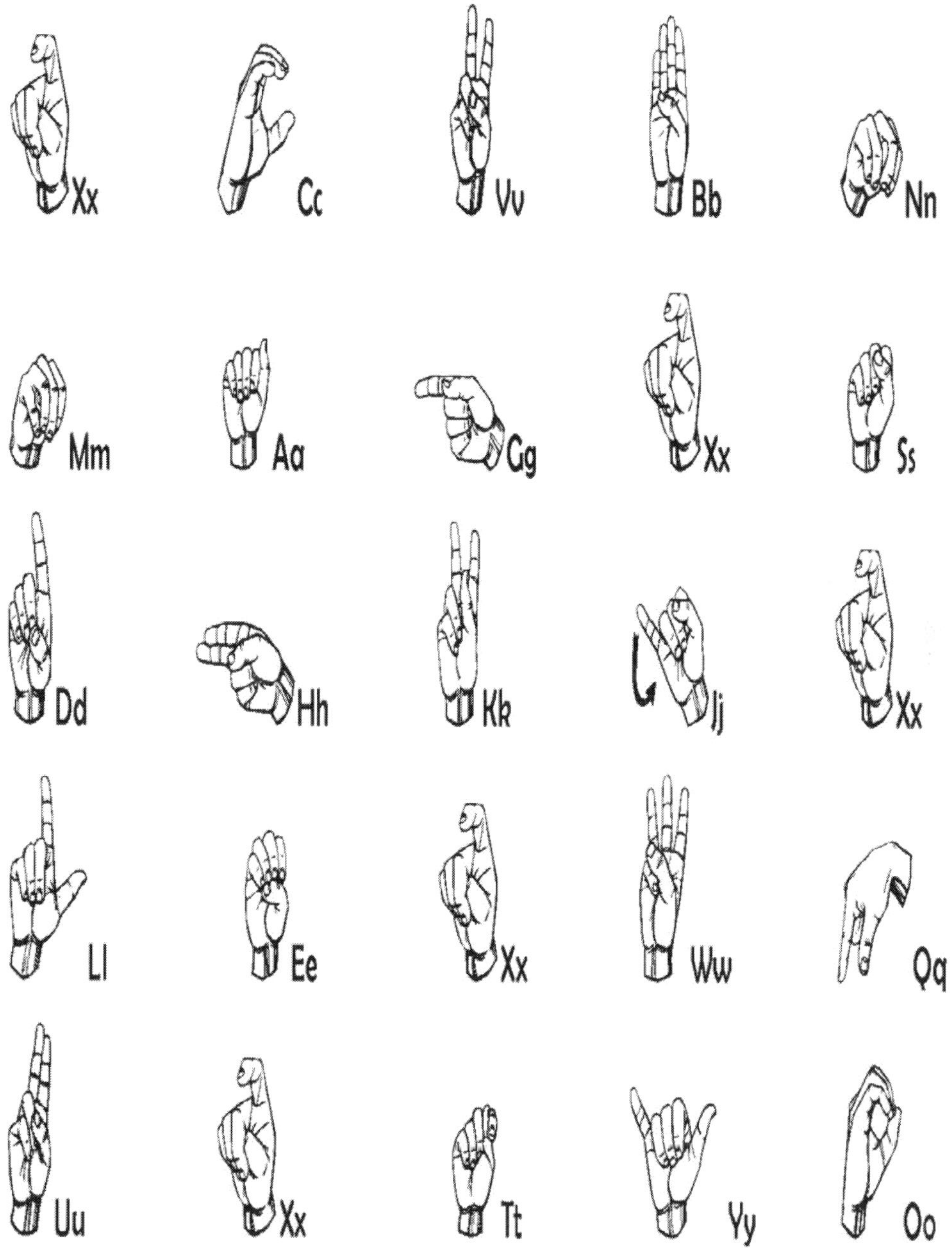

Xx	Cc	Vv	Bb	Nn
Mm	Aa	Gg	Xx	Ss
Dd	Hh	Kk	Jj	Xx
Ll	Ee	Xx	Ww	Qq
Uu	Xx	Tt	Yy	Oo

Name: _____

Review Page

Directions: Write the first letter of each word next to the picture.

Name: _____

Signing with Numbers

Directions: Draw a line connecting the number to the matching sign.

10

12

14

16

20

11

17

13

19

15

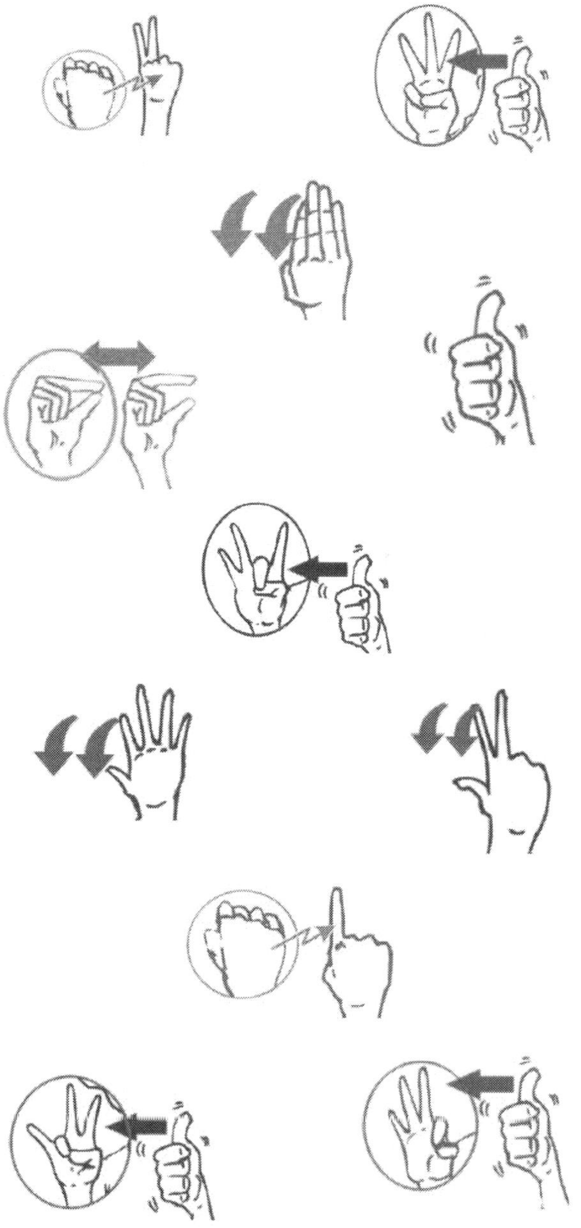

Yy

yo-yo

yack

Name: _____

Letter Search

Directions: Circle the letter Yy in the signlanguage letters below.

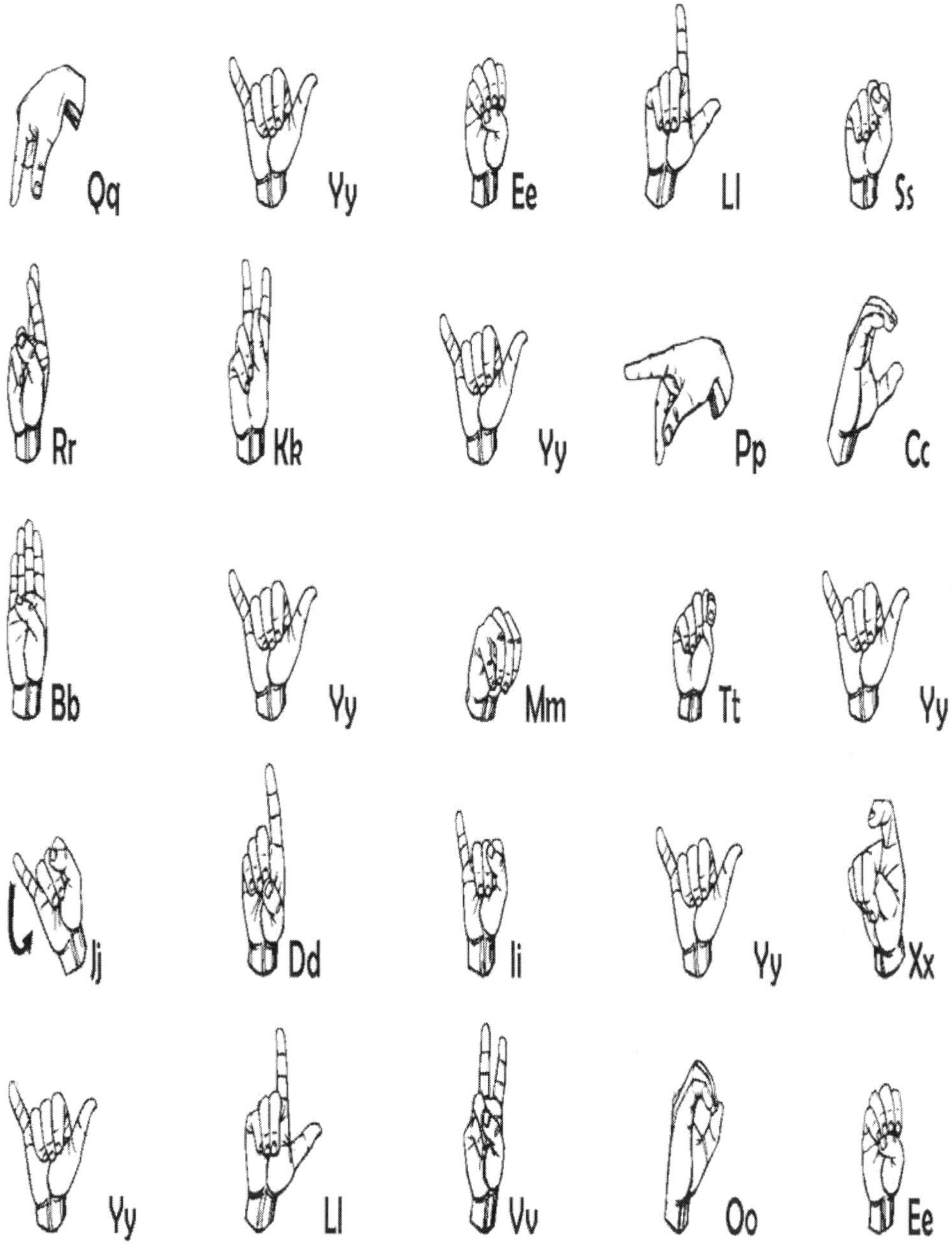

Qq	Yy	Ee	Ll	Ss
Rr	Kk	Yy	Pp	Cc
Bb	Yy	Mm	Tt	Yy
Jj	Dd	Ii	Yy	Xx
Yy	Ll	Vv	Oo	Ee

Zz

zipper

zebra

Name: _____

Zig-Zag Zebra

Directions: Draw z on the zebra to give it stripes.

Name: _____

Signing with Shapes

Directions: Draw a line connecting the sape with its sign.

86.

Name: _____

Amazing Alphabet

Directions: Fill in the missing letters of the alphabet

87.

Color Exercise Activity

Here is a great daily activity for everyone to do every day! Just follow along with the song and if you are wearing the color stand up and do your workout!
Sing to the tune of BINGO.

There was a color in English its black, in Spanish it is Negro.
Hop, Hop, Hop on one foot. Hop, Hop, Hop on one foot. Hop, Hop, Hop on one foot.
If you're wearing Black hop on one foot.

There was a color in English its Brown, in Spanish its Café.
Wiggle, Wiggle, Wiggle you fingers. Wiggle, Wiggle, Wiggle your fingers.
Wiggle, Wiggle, Wiggle your fingers. If you're wearing brown wiggle your fingers.

There was a color in English its Tan, in Spanish its bronceado.
Touch, Touch, Touch your toes. Touch, Touch, Touch your toes.
Touch, Touch, Touch your toes. If you're wearing brown touch your toes.

There was a color in English its Peach, in Spanish its Durazno.
Stretch, Stretch, Stretch your arms. Stretch, Stretch, Stretch your arms.
Stretch, Stretch, Stretch your arms. If you're wearing Peach Stretch your arms.

There was a color in English its Gold, in Spanish it is Oro.
Wave, Wave, Wave your hands. Wave, Wave, Wave your hands.
Wave, Wave, Wave your hands. If you're wearing Gold wave your hands.

There was a color in English its Silver, in Spanish it is Plata.
Squat, Squat, Squat your legs. Squat, Squat, Squat your legs.
Squat, Squat, Squat your legs. If you're wearing Silver squat your legs.

Color Exercise Activity Continued

There was a color in English its Red, in Spanish it is Rojo.
Turn, Turn, Turn around. Turn, Turn, Turn around.
Turn, Turn, Turn around. If you're wearing Red turn around.

There was a color in English its Pink, in Spanish its Rosa.
Shake, Shake, Shake your head. Shake, Shake, Shake your head.
Shake, Shake, Shake your head. If you're wearing Pink shake your head.

There was a color in English its Orange, in Spanish its Anaranjado.
March, March, March like a soldier. March, March, March like a soldier.
March, March, March like a soldier. If you're wearing orange march like a soldier.

There was a color in English its Gray, in Spanish it is Gris.
Pat, Pat, Pat your back. Pat, Pat, Pat your back. Pat, Pat, Pat your back.
If you're wearing gray pat your back.

There was a color in English its White, in Spanish it is Blanco.
Jump, Jump, Jump up and down. Jump, jump, jump up and down.
Jump, jump, jump up and down. If you're wearing white jump up and down.

There was a color in English it's Blue, in Spanish it is Azul.
Stomp, Stomp Stomp your feet. Stomp, stomp, stomp your feet.
Stomp, stomp, stomp your feet. If you're wearing blue stomp your feet.

Color Exercise Activity Continued

There was a color in English it's Yellow, in Spanish it's Amarillo.
Stand, Stand, on one foot. Stand, Stand on one foot.
Stand, Stand on one foot. If you're wearing yellow stand on one foot.

There was a color in English it's Purple, in Spanish it is Purpura.
Shake, Shake, Shake your shoulders. Shake, shake, shake your shoulders.
Shake, shake, shake your shoulders.
If you're wearing purple shake your shoulders.

There was a color in English it's Green, in Spanish it is Verde.
Jump, Jump, Jumping Jacks. Jump, jump, jumping jacks.
Jump, jump, jumping jacks. If you're wearing green do jumping jacks.

There are many colors in English it's a Rainbow, in Spanish it's Arco Iris.
Shake, shake, shake your hips. Shake, shake, shake your hips.
Shake, shake, shake your hips. If you're wearing rainbow colors shake your hips.

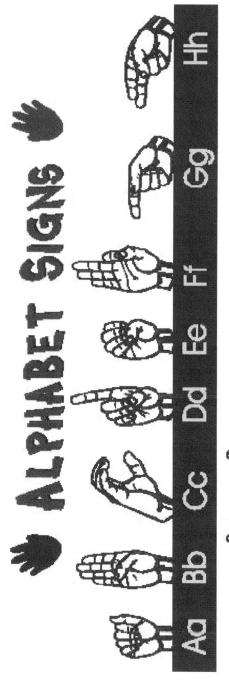

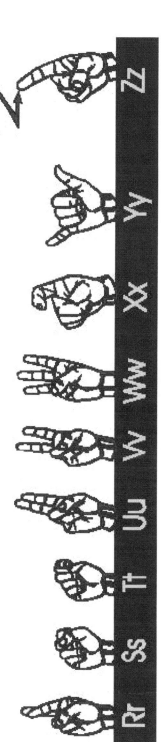

Made in the USA
Charleston, SC
20 December 2014